Workhorse Walter

Original Story
Created & Written by
Larry Jay Robinson

Workhorse Walter

First Edition © Copyright August 2020

Author ~ Larry Jay Robinson

Editor-in-Chief, Steve William Laible, MBA
Typist, Lauren Oliver
Interior Formatted by TKG

Published by The Kodel Group, LLC
Imprint: Empire Holdings
Literary Division for Young Readers
P.O. Box 38, Grants Pass, Oregon, USA 97528
KodelEmpire.com

Workhorse Walter is a work ethic and purpose story for children. Mr. Robinson's books are rich with adventure, lessons, discoveries, vibrant independence, peril and above all else, friendships. Larry's head is filled with stories that must be penned. This is 'his' new purpose.

Print ISBN-13: 978-1-62485-070-7
Kindle ISBN-13: 978-1-62485-072-1

Printed in the United States of America, Europe, Asia, and beyond.

Dedicated

to

Tradesmen and women who not only built
this great country but sustain her.

and

Journeymen who taught apprentices
their respective trades.

I salute you all.

“America became the greatest nation
on the planet because of a moral code;
work ethic; heroes and people who knew
what leadership and vision were.”

Steve William Laible
American Children’s Author

Workhorse Walter

This is a story about a horse named Walter. Walter was a big horse, a draft horse. He lived on a farm in a peaceful little valley.

Every day he woke up early, willing and able to work. Walter did all kinds of jobs around the farm. He pulled the plow when it was time to prepare the soil for crops. He pulled the wagon when it was time to go into town for supplies. He pulled logs out of the woods for firewood and lumber.

Walter liked to work—any kind of work. He lived to get dirty, feel the ground sigh beneath his powerful feet.

The brisk morning air was Walter's greeting each day and rain or shine Walter enjoyed his work. It's what he did. What he was born to do.

Day in and day out Walter kept busy doing his many jobs. Some days were routine but other days were quite challenging. Like the days Walter had to pull tree stumps out to clear more land for crops. Some stumps just didn't want to let go of their hold on the ground.

It was still fun to Walter though. It was hard work and work was what Walter lived for so therefore it was fun.

Year after year Walter did his job the best he could. He always worked longer days than any of the other horses on the farm.

In fact, most of the other horses didn't work at all. They were just there to be ridden or raced. Walter saw that as frivolous and the waste of a day that could be better spent working.

Walter was the largest, most respected horse on the farm. He could do any chore singlehandedly.

He and Fred, the farmer, worked well together and every morning Fred would say, "Good morning Walter, today we're going to go plow that new field we cleared." or "Good morning Walter, today we need to bring in some logs for lumber."

But one day Fred greeted Walter at his stable with a young draft horse in tow, "Good morning Walter. This is Musky. He's going to help us today."

"I never needed help before," thought Walter.

“I want you to help me show Musky how to do our work here. He'll be your partner,” said Fred.

“I don't need a partner," thought Walter, “I work alone."

Nonetheless Fred took the two horses down to the main field. There he hooked the two horses up to the plow with a yoke joining them together.

"Ah, hi,” said Musky, "I've heard a lot about you. My name is Musky."

"Yea, I heard. I don't need any help, and certainly not from some greenhorn wannabe." said Walter in horse talk.

But they were paired up with the yoke, so Walter had no choice but to work alongside this youngster.

"Try to keep up," said Walter.

When Fred gave the order to start, Walter moved but Musky didn't. The yoke yanked on Walter's neck.

"Come on!" he yelled at Musky.

That day became the first day in Walter's life that he didn't like going to work.

Walter looked back at Fred with pleading eyes as if to say, "Take this yoke off of me. I can't work with this guy."

"This contraption is going to help Musky learn," said Fred noticing Walter's displeasure.

"It will get better Walter. Come on now; let's show him how it's done."

Reluctantly Walter started again telling Musky, "One foot in front of the other," while thinking to himself, "This is going to be a long day.

Musky did his best to keep step with Walter and after a little herky jerky start they settled into a rhythm.

Sometime around mid-morning something must have clicked with the newbie because the yoke wasn't jerking on Walter's neck anymore.

The two horses were working well together. Walter had quit fighting the yoke and Musky quite fighting Walter.

“Now you’re working like a team,” said Fred, and Walter realized this WAS a little easier.

"Maybe a partner isn't such a bad idea,” thought Walter.

They got through the day and Walter looked back at how much they got done.

“I’ve done more than that in a day by myself,” he thought.

"It'll get better tomorrow," said Fred to Walter.

“I have to work with that horse again tomorrow? Great," thought Walter.

When they got back to the stable Musky asked Walter, "What do we do now?"

“WE don't do anything. I'M going to eat and take it easy. You can do whatever you want,” said Walter, “and don't think we're going to hang out together. It's bad enough I have to work with you."

“I thought we were friends,” said Musky, "we worked so well together.”

“There are two things wrong there," said Walter.

“First, we are not friends and second I've done more work than that by myself.”

So, Walter ate his usual meal, got himself a long drink of water and got comfortable in his stall in the stable.

Musky wandered around a bit.

Farmer Fred came around after dinner to put the horses in their stalls for the night.

Walter was already in his stall so Fred just closed the stall door and said, "Goodnight Walter. See you in the morning."

Musky was out in the corral checking out his new surroundings. Fred tracked him down and put him in his stall.

"Now you get some rest Musky. We've got more work to do tomorrow," said Fred before he left.

The next morning Walter was up at the crack of dawn, as usual, ready for another day of work. He looked over at the stall Musky was in and thought, "Darn, he really is here. I was hoping yesterday was just a bad dream."

Then Walter thought, “If I don't wake him up I won’t have to work with him."

Just then Farmer Fred walked into the barn.

“Good morning Walter," he said, "looks like I need to wake up Musky.”

"Please don't," thought Walter.

"Musky!" yelled Fred banging on the stall door.

Musky jumped to his feet, “I’m awake, I'm awake,” he said in horse talk.

"We get up early around here," said Walter (also in horse talk).

Farmer Fred led the two horses down to the main field and put the yoke back on them to start plowing.

"Let's try to do this right today," said Walter to Musky.

"Okay," said Musky, still trying to wake up.

This day the two worked better together as Musky made sure he just followed what Walter did.

They plowed through that field like a well-oiled machine and at the end of the day Walter said, "There, now look back at what we did today. That's more like it."

Musky was just glad he made it through the day without making any mistakes.

"This guy is a pretty fast learner, thought Walter, "but I'm not going to tell him that."

Day after day, week after week, month and month Walter taught the newbie how to do all the different jobs around the farm. Musky did learn fast and soon he mastered all the duties of his position.

One day Farmer Fred came into the barn and got Musky out of his stall first. He had never done that before, so Walter wondered what was going on.

"Walter," said Fred, "I'm taking Musky out solo today. You can take it easy."

Walter was not used to that. He was a work horse and his job was to work. He was confused. He had never NOT worked before.

While Fred worked Musky that day, Walter decided to visit some of the other horses.

"Hi guys," Walter said as he approached a group of racehorses exercising.

"Hi Walter," said one of them. "Hi Walter," said another, "Why aren't you working?"

"Are you feeling alright?" asked another.

"Yea, I feel fine," said Walter, "Fred is taking Musky out solo today."

"Oh," said one of the horses, "you know what that means don't you?"

"It means I have a day off," said Walter.

"When have you ever had a day off Walter?" said one horse.

"You've been replaced," said another.

"You're going to be put out to pasture. Your working days are over," said another.

"I have to work," said Walter, "it's what I do."

"Get used to retirement" said one of the horses.

"I don't want to retire," said Walter as he walked away. "Why would they even say that," he thought, "I've worked as long as I can remember."

As he was headed back to his stall he saw Musky pulling the plow that he used to pull.

“I guess I should have known,” he thought, "I am getting older. I just don't know what to do with myself now. How do I fill the day?"

Walter turned and started walking back to the barn.

The school bus had arrived to drop off the kids. Walter watched as the kids got off the bus and it drove away.

"Hey," said one of the neighborhood kids named Bobby, "Look at that horse. He's huge!"

"That's our horse Walter," said little Vera.

"How come I never seen him before?" asked Bobby.

"He's usually plowing the fields or bringing in hay, or pulling out logs.

He's always working," said Vera.

"Can you ride him?" asked Bobby.

"I don't know," said Vera as her mom walked up. "Mom, can we ride Walter?"

"I don't know that he's ever been ridden honey. Walter is a work horse," said Vera's mom, Mrs. Chatfield.

"Why is he out? Why isn't he working mom?" Vera asked.

"He's being put out to pasture," Vera's mom answered.

"What does that mean Mrs. Chatfield?" asked Bobby.

"He won't have to work anymore," she replied.

"What's he gonna do mom?" asked Vera.

"I really don't know. I guess we hadn't thought that much about it. Walter has been a dependable work horse for so many years. I suppose it might feel funny to him to not be working," she said.

"Do you think we could ride him Mrs. Chatfield?" Bobby asked.

"Yea mom, can we?" asked Vera.

"Let's talk to your father at dinner tonight, said Mrs. Chatfield. "Can we pet him Mrs. Chatfield? asked Bobby.

"I don't see why not," she said and then took the kids to see Walter.

Walter saw them approach and wondered what was up. He had never been around kids and wasn't quite sure how to take this.

“Hi Walter," said Mrs. Chatfield when she got closer, “the kids wanted to come see you."

“He's so big,” said Bobby.

"Let him smell your hand," said Vera, then maybe you can pet him."

Walter sniffed at Bobby's hand, “No food? Hmm, he seems harmless enough," he thought as he lowered his head as if to say, “Scratch my neck."

Bobby responded by petting Walter's neck and Walter stood there like the gentle giant he was.

"He's so cool," said Bobby, "Please talk to your dad tonight. I'm going to go tell my parents I made friends with a giant horse." Bobby ran all the way home he was so excited.

"He sure is happy," said Mrs. Chatfield.

"He's never seen a horse like Walter before," said Vera.

"Walter is something special," said Vera's mom.

That night at dinner Vera could hardly contain herself and as soon as the prayer was done she blurted out, "Daddy today Bobby and I saw Walter. Are you putting him out to pasture?"

"Yes. Walter's worked a lot of years. It's time for him to live out his days without working," said farmer Fred.

"Since he won't be working anymore can we ride him?" asked Vera.

"Never really thought about it," said Fred.

“He was really good with the kids today," said Mrs. Chatfield.

"He's quite big. And he's wide,” said Fred.

"They don't usually make saddles that big.”

“Please daddy," said Vera batting her eyes.

“I have to have a special saddle made,” he replied.

“Please daddy," she said again.

"You sure do know my weakness, don't you?" he said to Vera.

"Sure. I'll get a saddle made. In the meantime, you and Bobby get to know Walter a little better. Take him an apple after school, or a carrot. Get him to trust you and watch out for those big feet of his."

"Thank you, Daddy," said Vera grinning from ear to ear.

So, the next day after school Vera and Bobby took some apples to Walter and spent time with him.

"Dad's making a special saddle so we can ride you Walter," said Vera.

"And I can't wait" said Bobby.

"What are these kids talking about," Walter wondered as he ate the apples.

A few days later while the kids were with Walter a man came over with farmer Fred and took a lot of measurements on Walter.

"Are these the kids you want the saddle made for?" the man asked Fred.

"Yes," said Fred.

"How old are you guys," the man asked.

"I'm seven," said Vera.

"I'm almost eight," said Bobby.

The man sized up the kids and then took Fred aside. "How many more years do you suppose Walter has left?" he asked.

"Five or six, maybe more," said Fred.

"Okay," said the man, "I want to make you a saddle the kids can still use as they grow."

"That sounds good. And since he's so wide, can you make one they could both ride at the same time?" asked Fred.

“That's exactly what I was thinking," said the man, “it won't look like your standard saddle and it won't be cheap.”

"I didn't expect it to be. You know me, I don't want cheap. I want quality," said Fred.

"The man left, and the kids asked when the saddle would be done.

"Mr. Chatfield," said Bobby, "How long will it take him to build a saddle for Walter."

"I'm not sure Bobby, it's going to be a special saddle," said Farmer Fred.

While the kids waited for the saddle, Walter was also waiting—waiting for the school bus to drop off the kids.

When Musky took over Walter's job around the farm it left a void in Walter's life. It seemed like his purpose in life was gone, but now, with the kids, he felt he had a new purpose.

He enjoyed his time with the kids and it gave him a reason to look forward to each new day.

When the saddle finally arrived, it was indeed unlike other saddles. It was more of a seat and wide enough for two kids to fit in.

Farmer Fred built a special ladder for the kids to climb up to get on the seat on Walter's back. It was quite secure, safe, and comfortable.

Vera and Bobby climbed up and into the saddle seat.

Farmer Fred gave the two some instructions on how to lead Walter.

"He's quite smart," said Fred, "He knows all the verbal commands like, Go, Stop, Right, Left and Back. You can work the reigns also but it's not necessary if you talk to him."

"Mr. Chatfield, *Whoa* means stop, right?" asked Bobby.

"Yes, or slow down." said Fred.

"I can see the whole world up here," said Bobby.

Farmer Fred led them out to the pasture to get used to the new saddle and how it felt to ride on Walter.

“Looks like you're back at work Walter," said Fred.

Walter was happy to hear the word ‘work’ again although it didn't seem much like work until Fred added, "You're carrying precious cargo Walter. Make sure they come back in one piece."

Now Walter felt responsible for the safety of his riders. It sounded even more like work now, and Walter was quite comfortable with that, after all, he was a work horse.

It didn't take long for the kids to get used to riding Walter and it didn't take Walter long to get used to the kids.

Before too long more kids were coming over to ride Walter. Either Vera or Bobby would take each new kid on a ride.

Bobby even brought over his handicapped brother, Shane. It was a joy to everyone to see his face light up when he was atop this gentle giant of a horse.

Shane didn't usually show much emotion so that got Mrs. Chatfield to thinking that perhaps other handicapped or disabled children would also enjoy riding Walter.

Soon Walter had more friends than he could have imagined and some of the children had emotional breakthroughs. Some parents said it was the first time they had seen their child smile. One little girl even said her first word, "Walter."

It was a win-win situation! Walter had something important to do again and the children got to experience something new and stimulating.

While Walter was unknowingly becoming a “therapy horse" Musky was busy doing all of Walter's old jobs. He was doing quite a good job also. He had had a good teacher.

However, one day while Musky and farmer Fred were out logging a tree faller had just about finished his cut when the tree turned on its stump and fell the wrong way.

The wayward tree brought down other trees with it pinning Musky and Fred underneath the pile.

The faller ran over to find them both hopelessly trapped, "Are you okay?” he asked Fred, "Where are you? I can't see you.”

“I’m okay,” said Fred from under the debris, “I just can't move. I've got branches all around me. Go get Walter and get these trees off of us.”

“Yes sir,” said the tree faller and then he hustled back to the farm. He found Walter entertaining the kids as they were taking turns riding.

"Help!" the faller yelled as he got there, "There's been an accident. I need Walter.”

A farmhand came over and helped the kids get to the ladder and get off of Walter. Then he helped get the special saddle off.

“Come on Walter,” said the faller, "we need to get rope and get back to the woods.”

Once he had the rope he hopped on Walter and said, “Let’s go boy.”

"Hold on tight,” said Walter in horse talk as he started running toward the woods.

When they got there, Walter saw the pile of fallen trees that was trapping Musky and Fred underneath.

The faller started cutting branches and Walter dragged them away.

Soon, another farmhand showed up and as the faller cut bigger logs, he helped Walter pull them aside. It was hard work and they worked as fast as they could.

"We're almost there Fred," said the faller, “Just a couple more branches.”

With a few more cuts and branches dragged away, Fred and Musky pulled themselves from the debris. They both had only minor injuries and no broken bones.

"Thank you, Walter. Thank you, guys. If it wasn't for you and Walter, I'd have been stuck there all night."

"I'm just glad I could help and that you're alright," thought Walter.

“Thanks,” said Musky in horse talk, "you still got it old man.”

"You're welcome," said Walter, "besides, I had to do it. You have work to do."

Everybody went back to the farm, “we'll clean that mess up tomorrow,” said Fred, “all of us need some rest."

The next day Fred and Musky went back to the woods to finish up, and Walter, well he got to sleep in a little and then watch for the school bus.

"I like my new job," he told himself as he waited for the kids—and the apples, of course.

The End

Other Books by this Author

Stubborn Stanley
Runaway Buster
Tomatoes are Poison

www.ingramcontent.com/pod-product-compliance
Lightning Source LLC
La Vergne TN
LVHW010548100826
845148LV00013B/2660

* 9 7 8 1 6 2 4 8 5 0 7 0 7 *